Key IMMIGRATION LAWS

Cavendish Square
New York

Kathryn Ohnaka

Published in 2020 by Cavendish Square Publishing, LLC

243 5th Avenue, Suite 136, New York, NY 10016

Copyright © 2020 by Cavendish Square Publishing, LLC

First Edition

Website: cavendishsq.com

This publication represents the opinions and views of the author based on his or her personal experience, knowledge, and research. The information in this book serves as a general guide only. The author and publisher have used their best efforts in preparing this book and disclaim liability rising directly or indirectly from the use and application of this book.

All websites were available and accurate when this book was sent to press.

Cataloging-in-Publication Data

Names: Ohnaka, Kathryn.
Title: Key immigration laws / Kathryn Ohnaka.
Description: New York : Cavendish Square Publishing, 2020. | Series: Laws that changed history | Includes glossary and index.
Identifiers: ISBN 9781502655264 (pbk.) | ISBN 9781502655271 (library bound) | ISBN 9781502655288 (ebook)
Subjects: LCSH: Emigration and immigration law--United States--Juvenile literature.
Classification: LCC KF4819.85 O36 2020 | DDC 342.7308'2--dc23

Printed in China

Photo Credits: Cover, p. 1 pisaphotography/Shutterstock.com; p. 5 Edwin Levick/Hulton Archive/Getty Images; pp. 8-9 David McNew/Getty Images; p. 10 Lambert/Hulton Fine Art Collection/Getty Images; p. 13 DEA Picture Library/De Agostini/Getty Images; pp. 14-15 PhotoQuest/Archive Photos/Getty Images; p. 17 Lordprice Collection/Alamy Stock Photo; pp. 20-21 © AP Images; pp. 22-23 Universal History Archive/Universal Images Group/Getty Images; p. 25 Nicholas Kamm/AFP/Getty Images; pp. 28, 40-41 Everett Historical/Shutterstock.com; p. 31 nsf/Alamy Stock Photo; pp. 32-33 Rena Schild/Shutterstock.com; p. 38 Christopher Furlong/Getty Images; pp. 42-43 John Moore/Getty Images; pp. 44-45 Bryan R. Smith/Getty Images; p. 48 Africa Studio/Shutterstock.com; p. 49 Drew Angerer/Getty Images; p. 51 AFP/Getty Images; pp. 52-53 Herika Martinez/AFP/Getty Images; pp. 56-57 Orlok/Shutterstock.com; pp. 58-59 David McNew/Getty Images; pp. 62-63 Justin Sullivan/Getty Images; pp. 64-65 AhXiong/Shutterstock.com; cover, back cover, and interior pages Capitol dome graphic Alexkava/Shutterstock.com.

CONTENTS

Introduction

Who belongs here? It's a question Americans have asked since before the United States officially became a country. For centuries, immigrants from all over the world have flocked to America's shores, seeking safety, jobs, freedom, and better lives for themselves and their families. Some have been welcomed and others scorned, but as the years pass, more immigrants arrive. The country's laws continue to grow and change as its population becomes more diverse.

The government works to adjust the laws as immigrants arrive. In 2019, the focus was on immigrants from Mexico and Central America as well as predominantly Muslim countries in Africa and the Middle East. On September 24, 2017, President Donald Trump signed an executive order stating that visa applications would not be accepted from Iran, Yemen, Somalia, Syria, Libya, and North Korea. It was the third version of the order, often referred to as "the Muslim Ban." Earlier versions had included additional Muslim-majority countries.[1]

In the early 1900s, many immigrants came to the United States by crossing the Atlantic Ocean, sailing past the Statue of Liberty on the way to Ellis Island.

President Trump claimed that this ban would reduce terrorism and crime in the United States. Opponents said the act discriminated against people of the Muslim faith. The various versions of the order were challenged in court, but the third version was ultimately upheld by the Supreme Court. It ruled that under the Immigration and Nationality Act, the ban protects America's interests. Opponents continue to challenge the ban.

This isn't the first ban on nationalities of people. European, African, and Chinese people have faced similar bans throughout history. People argued that these immigrants would disrupt the culture, steal jobs, or consume resources. These bans were protested and overturned, and new laws were created to ensure immigrants could stay. It sometimes took decades, but every time the laws changed, America's culture became more diverse.

Why are so many people coming to the United States? Some seek freedom from tyrannical governments or religious persecution. Some flee violence, war, or natural disasters. Some are starving, in need of medical care, or want to be reunited with family. Some seek education or better lives for their children. The United States promises freedom from tyranny, freedom of speech and religion, and ample resources. Once they arrive, immigrants need to apply either for asylum or for a visa or green card. Immigrants are guaranteed a hearing to see if they can stay, but getting to these hearings can take years. The process is arduous, but many people feel that the chance at life in America is worth it.

For centuries, immigrants have come to America in hopes of finding a better life—a life of freedom and hope promised by the US Constitution. Laws have changed through history to accommodate them. Let's look at these laws and how they've affected people throughout America's history.

Who Are Immigrants?

Immigrants are people born in a foreign country who wish to live elsewhere. They pack their belongings, leave everything they've ever known, and move to a new country to seek a new life. Immigrants to the United States come from all over the world.

Immigrants can become citizens, or they can live in America on a resident visa—a certificate or stamp in a person's passport that allows them to stay in the country. If an immigrant wishes to keep their own country's citizenship but live and work in the United States, they are required to have a green card, which is a special permit that can be renewed repeatedly.[1] Specific rights are granted by certain visas; for example, an immigrant on a student visa is allowed to study in America, but not to work. Immigrants who are not citizens are sometimes referred to as "aliens." If they enter the country legally, they are referred to as documented; if not, they are undocumented.

Immigrants can enter the country legally for a variety of reasons. They may be marrying an American citizen, seeking

Immigrants can enter the United States for a variety of reasons, including seeking political asylum, getting an education, or marrying a US citizen.

work, seeking to be reunited with family, wanting to study, or wanting to travel for an extended period of time. Others may be seeking asylum, which is when a person flees from their home country to escape war, a disaster, a tyrannical government, or religious persecution. People who enter illegally generally either sneak in over the border or overstay their visa, meaning they stay past the visa's expiration date. Undocumented immigrants enter the country largely for the same reasons that legal immigrants do but are frequently in too much danger at home to wait for the proper permission. All immigrants, documented or not, are guaranteed basic protections and rights under the US Constitution and its amendments.

The Earliest Immigrants

Before the days of visas, anyone who had the ability to get on a boat could immigrate to America. The first immigrants to America came from Europe. They began arriving in the

The Pilgrims left England, seeking a new land where they could make their own laws—a land where they would have religious and political freedoms.

1500s from England, France, and Spain, and they set up small colonies. Explorers came looking for land and gold. The journey was expensive and arduous, and many did not survive. Those who did live found that the land was far different from Europe, dangerous and difficult to colonize, as there were already people living there. Many Native Americans were killed by colonizers.

One of the most famous groups of early immigrants was the Pilgrims, who came from England in 1620 seeking freedom from the king. As they sought a new life, they hoped for religious freedom, freedom from strict laws and taxes, and a new government. They had grown tired of England's strict religious laws and what they felt was overreach from the king. Over the next twenty years, some 20,000 Puritans settled on the East Coast, looking to establish their own religious colonies.[2] More settlers followed in hopes of finding work or owning their own land.

Many of the colonies were set up like communities had been in England. This meant that white, male landowners were allowed some voting rights. Many early immigrants were enticed by the idea of having some say in their local governments, and land was available and cheap.[3] This meant many immigrants could become landowners and acquire the

"Person" vs. "Citizen" in the Constitution: What's the Difference?

The Constitution begins "We the People." Many of the amendments use the same language. "People" means all humans on American soil, while "citizen" refers to a person who was born in the United States or a person who has gone through the citizenship process. The Supreme Court decided in 1886 during a case called *Yick Wo v. Hopkins* that all people within the territorial jurisdiction of the United States—not just citizens—would be protected by the due process clause of the Fourteenth Amendment, which was ratified in 1868 and says that neither the federal government nor the state governments may deprive a person of life, liberty, or property without a proper trial.[4]

right to vote. Immigration to America was not regulated, so anyone who had the money could immigrate.

Not all settlers were willing immigrants. Europe reduced its criminal population by sending convicts to be servants in the colonies. People were kidnapped and forced to work on ships or as servants in America. These people were not considered citizens or immigrants in the legal sense, and they did not have the same rights.

Most of the unwilling immigrants were slaves brought from Africa. By the late 1600s, there were about 7,000 slaves in the colonies. By the time the US Constitution was written in 1789, there were estimated to be about 700,000 slaves. Slaves are people who are the property of others, forced to work without any kind of compensation. The government did not consider slaves to be immigrants or citizens, and they had no rights under the US Constitution or its amendments.[5]

The Constitution, Amendments, and Acts

In the late 1700s, the king of England began to raise taxes on the colonies and impose restrictions on them. Frustrated with the British government, the settlers revolted, declared their independence, and successfully fought the British in the Revolutionary War. Once the former colonies became their own country, they needed their own government. A group of congressional delegates called the Framers, which included Benjamin Franklin, George Washington, and Alexander Hamilton, came together to create America's Constitution, the first set of laws.

The US Constitution is a contract between the government and the people. It is the supreme law of the land and overrides state and local laws. As the country grew and changed, people realized the US Constitution didn't fully meet their needs, so they changed, or amended, it.[6] Amendments are changes to the US Constitution

Alexander Hamilton was one of the country's Founding Fathers. He was part of the group that conceived of and drafted the Constitution.

that are approved both by Congress and by at least three-quarters of the states. As of 2019, the US Constitution has twenty-seven amendments.

The first ten amendments are called the Bill of Rights. They were originally written by James Madison to protect the rights of the people. They guarantee freedom of speech and press; the right to bear arms; the right for people to have their homes protected from search and seizure and from being used as

The idea of freedoms relating to religion, speech, and happiness drew countless people to America's shores in the early twentieth century. Ellis Island, New York, is where many immigrants from Europe arrived.

soldiers' quarters; the right to a jury trial and to be free of cruel and unusual punishments; and that states may make their own laws as long as they do not conflict with the US Constitution.[7]

In addition to the US Constitution and the amendments, there are other laws called acts. Acts are not part of the US Constitution; unlike amendments, they often have time limits attached and can expire. They can be modified by the government relatively easily if circumstances change or if the people find the acts do not work as well as they could. They can also be cancelled entirely. Immigrants must follow all US laws.

Many immigrants were enticed by the ideas of freedom of speech, freedom of religion, and the right to seek their own happiness. As word continued to spread, the immigrant population became more diverse in its nationalities and backgrounds. In the 1700s, the immigrants were primarily European; in the following centuries, immigrants would come from other parts of Europe, Africa, Asia, and South America.

The US Constitution and its amendments did not apply to everyone: Rights were only given to white, male landowners. Women, people of color, and slaves did not receive all rights immediately. Black people were not given rights until after the American Civil War, when the Fourteenth Amendment was adopted in 1868. Over time, immigrants used the amendments in Supreme Court cases to petition for inclusion in the laws. As more immigrants came from a more diverse group of countries, the laws were challenged and changed to accommodate them. It was not easy: Each group of immigrants had to fight for their rights to be recognized.

Nationality and Immigration

The 1800s and 1900s saw a massive increase in immigration in the United States. Immigrants arrived from other countries in Europe, followed by Asian and South American immigrants. Many people who had arrived in the country earlier resisted immigration, and many laws were passed in an attempt to control who could enter the country. These included quotas, bans, and restrictions, many of which have been argued about and reformed for decades. Much of the argument involved trying to determine which immigrants were best for America, based on the countries they came from.

The 1800s: The Debate Begins

In the 1800s, groups of Irish immigrants packed themselves into boats to come to America. The conditions were terrible. Overcrowding and poor health led to outbreaks of typhus, cholera, and dysentery. When the immigrants disembarked, they were often met with angry outcries from US citizens,

Many Americans resisted the arrival of unemployed Irish immigrants, fearing their own jobs would be taken.

who feared immigrants would take their jobs or resources. Immigrants often lived in poor, filthy conditions in the cities, struggling to survive.[1] Why would they want to come to such a country?

Often, immigrants had been starving in their home countries. Around 1815, there was a surge in immigration. About half of the new immigrants were Irish. They left Ireland due to famine and came to America in search of food and jobs. German settlers came as well, creating settlements in the Midwest.[2] They created their own communities and tried to build a new life far from home.

As more and more groups from Europe arrived on America's shores, anti-immigrant feeling surged. From 1845 to 1854, 2.9 million immigrants arrived, and they didn't bring many resources with them.

Starting over was difficult, and many of the Irish immigrants needed government social services to survive. Because of their reliance on social services and their Catholic faith (in predominantly Protestant communities), many Irish immigrants faced strong opposition from established American citizens. Many Americans felt that the immigrants were a drain on their communities and a threat to the Protestant majority.

Around this time, a secret group calling themselves the "Know-Nothing Party" formed that was devoted to slowing Irish immigration.[3] The name was used because if an outsider asked them about their activities, they promised to reply, "I know nothing." A new political party formed from this group called the American Party, which ran on an anti-immigration and anti-Catholic platform. Throughout the 1850s, members of the party were vocal about deporting immigrants as a means of protecting their own culture and lifestyle. The party was short-lived, but the movement was strong.

The idea that immigrants threaten the lifestyle and culture of native-born people is called nativism, and it's an idea that has been pervasive throughout history in many countries. It differs slightly from nationalism, which is supporting one's country and culture over others.

In America in the 1850s, Chinese immigrants began to arrive to build railroads, which were becoming increasingly more desirable since the California gold rush began. Many Americans worried that Chinese and Catholic immigrants would disrupt their culture and take their land and jobs. This overwhelming sense of nativism contributed to the creation of the Naturalization Act of 1870, which said that only immigrants from Europe and Africa could become citizens; Asian immigrants could not. At this time, Congress rejected a proposal made by Massachusetts Senator Charles Sumner that would open naturalization for all immigrants. In 1885, the Alien Contract Labor Law said that employers could not bring over immigrants by promising them jobs.[4] This curbed immigration while at the same time supporting the American labor unions. Many felt the laws did not go far enough.

The 1882 Chinese Exclusion Act

One of the strongest immigration laws was the 1882 Chinese Exclusion Act. It was a ban on Chinese immigrants and, eventually, Asian immigrants overall.

Many Chinese laborers arrived to work in industry, agriculture, and to build railroads to aid America's westward expansion. They were often forced to work for lower wages than their native-born counterparts. Chinese immigrants often created their own settlements, known as Chinatowns, many of which remain today. They often had their own local cultures in these communities and their own rules. Americans in surrounding communities began to resent them and to

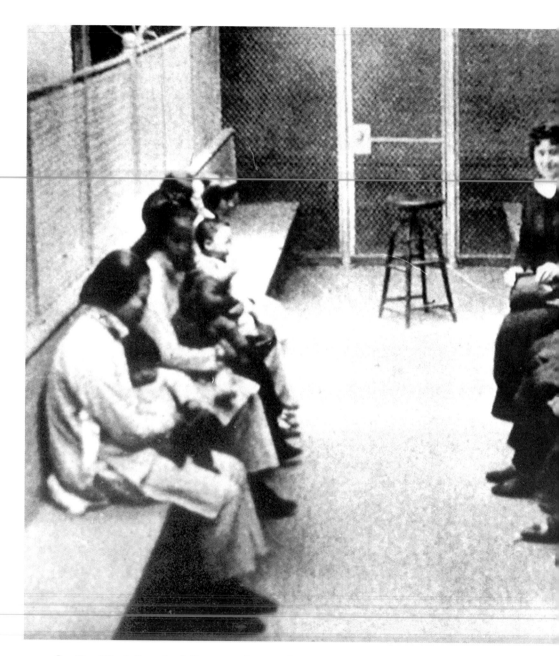

On the West Coast of the country, early twentieth-century Chinese and Japanese immigrants landed at Angel Island in San Francisco Bay, where they were often held in cells as they awaited processing.

think that the communities were corrosive to American communities. Nativism surged, and many people worked to restrict Chinese immigration. California began requiring Chinese immigrants to carry special licenses.

President Chester A. Arthur signed the 1882 Chinese Exclusion Act, which said no new immigrants from China could enter the country for ten years, and all those already in America had to carry a special license. It also placed a tax on each immigrant arriving, and it blocked convicts and "less intelligent" people from entering. Despite challenges made by Chinese workers already in the United States, the act remained and was extended for another ten years by the 1892 Geary Act, which also required that Chinese people carry identification certificates or face deportation.

The act was renewed multiple times, and it caused relations between America and China to weaken. The act was finally repealed in 1943.[5]

The 1900s: Quotas

In 1891, the Bureau of Immigration was created to decide how best to deal with immigrants. The immigration station at Ellis

During World War I, some German Americans were detained or deported because of American concerns about Germany's role in the war. The same happened with the Japanese during World War II.

Island opened on January 1, 1892. About 12 million immigrants passed through the station over the next sixty-two years. Many came from Europe, especially during World War I. As the war ended, paranoia rose about communists corrupting American politics. This panic, called the First Red Scare, caused many immigrants to be detained under suspicion of communism. Hundreds were deported.[6]

Around this time, the government enacted the National Origins Quota System, also known as the Immigration Act of 1924. The quota system allowed for a set number of visas per country, and once the visas were given out, no more immigrants could enter from that country. There were no visas allotted to Asian countries. All immigrants had to pass a literacy test.

The next immigration law was the Immigration and Nationality Act of 1952, also known as the McCarran-Walter Act. The act continued the quota system, but it ended Asian exclusion.[7] It added a merit system, prioritizing people with special skills or family already in America. It also increased the number of visas: most of them were allotted to Europeans, with a small number for Asians. One major change was that a foreign spouse of an American citizen could immigrate regardless of the quota, which made immigration easier for many people.

The quota system finally ended with the Hart-Cellar Act, also known as the Immigration and Nationality Act of 1965. Southern and Eastern European immigrants claimed the quota system discriminated against them because they were allowed fewer visas.

President John F. Kennedy agreed with them. He pushed for the new law, though it was ultimately his successor, Lyndon Johnson, who signed it, since Kennedy was assassinated in 1963. The new act removed the quotas, and it prioritized relatives of US citizens and permanent residents, people with special skills, and people seeking asylum from violence in their own country. Immigrant families began to arrive as family reunification became a major focus.[8] South American and Asian immigrants began to arrive as well. The act continues to affect America today.

The Immigration Reform and Control Act of 1986, signed into law by President Ronald Reagan, had several effects.[9] It granted amnesty to undocumented immigrants and agricultural workers who met certain conditions and had entered the United States before January 1, 1982; put sanctions on people who knowingly hired undocumented workers; and increased border enforcement. This was modified by the Immigration Act of 1990, which increased the overall number of immigrants and encouraged immigration from underrepresented countries to increase diversity.

In 1996, Congress passed the Illegal Immigration Reform and Immigrant Responsibility Act, which is still in effect as

Nationalism Today

"America first!" President Trump declared in his inaugural address. It became the rallying cry of many modern nationalists. In recent times, politics has blurred the lines between nationalism and nativism. Many people believe in protecting America's culture from foreign influences.

The 2017 travel ban and the detainment of undocumented aliens from Latin America are two of the results that stem from the idea that American interests must be protected over the interests of anyone else. In more extreme cases, nationalism in the United States has become white nationalism, a form of white supremacy that says that people who are not white are not "true" Americans and are harming American society. Many things drive this extremist form of nationalism: fear of losing jobs or a weak economy, fear of rising crime, and feeling that the country they're proud of is changing or lost.[10]

Under President Trump, nationalism has seen a return to politics, as he puts forward policies that focus on America and America alone.

25

of 2019. This act created penalties for immigrants if they overstayed their visa or entered the country without one, or if they committed a crime. If caught, they can be deported.[11] In 2002, the Homeland Security Act created the Department of Homeland Security (DHS), which took over many responsibilities of the Immigration Bureau.

The diversity of immigrants continued to increase. Between 1965 and 2000, most of the immigrants to the United States—an estimated 4.3 million—came from Mexico. About 1 million came from the Philippines, while 4 million other immigrants came from Korea, the Dominican Republic, India, Cuba, and Vietnam.[12]

As diversity and the number of immigrants increases, the argument about who belongs in the United States continues. The debate especially rages on about Mexican, Central American, and Middle Eastern immigrants. In 2017, Presidential Proclamation 9645, also called the "Muslim Ban," halted visa applications from Iran, Libya, Syria, Somalia, Yemen, North Korea, and some from Venezuela. Mexican and Central American immigrants, some seeking asylum, have been stopped at the border and detained as America struggles with how best to deal with them. We continue to examine our laws and how best to adapt them as immigration increases.

The Thirteenth and Fourteenth Amendments

At the end of the American Civil War, the United States faced a new issue. Hundreds of thousands of people who were neither citizens nor immigrants were living in the country; up until that point, they had been slaves and considered property, not people. They could not be sent to Africa because many of them came from families that had been living in the United States for generations. They were not immigrants to be deported; there was no life waiting for them in another country. The country had a new challenge and had to come up with laws to meet their needs. These laws would, in turn, benefit all immigrants.

A Unique Immigration Problem

On January 1, 1863, Abraham Lincoln issued the Emancipation Proclamation, declaring that all slaves in the Confederate states were free. However, it did not apply throughout the whole country, and it wasn't specifically a law; in fact, many Southern states ignored it. Despite these limitations, it still created a peculiar problem for the United States. How could

President Lincoln declared slavery over with the Emancipation Proclamation, but a new question arose: Were freed slaves citizens?

the government classify the newly freed slaves? How could they be properly integrated into the population? Were they citizens or immigrants?

In 1865, the government implemented the Thirteenth Amendment. The amendment says: "Neither slavery nor involuntary servitude, except as a punishment for crime whereof the party shall have been duly convicted, shall exist within the United States, or any place subject to their jurisdiction." This means that all people in America are free unless they have been convicted of a crime.[1]

Despite the proclamation and the amendment, African Americans still faced challenges. Most slaveowners didn't want to free their slaves or allow them to have the same rights as whites. Therefore, Congress enacted the Civil Rights Act of 1866, which said that "all persons born in the United States are hereby declared to be citizens of the United States," though Native Americans were not included in the act.[2]

President Andrew Johnson vetoed the law, but enough members of the House and Senate voted for it to override Johnson's veto. Still, lawmakers were concerned that the law wasn't strong enough. They thought a constitutional amendment would be a more effective way to enforce the citizenship rights of African Americans. Two months after passing the Civil Rights Act, Congress drafted the Fourteenth Amendment. It was meant to give black people citizenship, enforce their civil rights, and punish the Confederate states.

The Fourteenth Amendment states: "All persons born or naturalized in the United States and subject to the jurisdiction thereof, are citizens of the United States and of the State wherein they reside. No State shall make or enforce any law which shall abridge the privileges or immunities of citizens of the United States; nor shall any State deprive any person of life, liberty, or property, without due process of law; nor deny to any person within its jurisdiction the equal protection of the laws."[3]

This means that all people born on American soil are automatically citizens and are guaranteed the rights laid out by the US Constitution and the Bill of Rights. They are all to be given due process, or the right to a fair trial. The amendment includes an equal protection clause. It means that every state must govern all of its people equally, and it was designed to keep the formerly Confederate states from discriminating against black people.[4]

While the amendment also says that laws and courts must be equal, discriminatory laws were still acceptable. That meant individuals could still be discriminated against, such as under the "separate but equal" laws that provided separate—generally unequal—facilities for black people. It was also considered acceptable to ban certain groups of immigrants; immigrants entering the country were not citizens, and therefore not protected under the law. Immigrants benefited from the law in that once they entered the country, if they had a child on American soil, that child was automatically an American citizen. That child was afforded rights under the US Constitution and the amendments. As of 2019, this law is still in place.

When the amendment says, "nor shall any State deprive any person of life, liberty, or property, without due process of law; nor deny to any person within its jurisdiction the equal protection of the laws," there is a key distinction: "people" versus "citizens." The amendment specifically says "people," not "citizens," are given rights and due process.[5] "People" refers to everyone on American soil, not just citizens. This includes all immigrants, whether they entered the country legally or illegally. The government can't take anyone's belongings, put them in prison for an extended period of time, or put them to death without a fair trial in which it's proven the person did something wrong.

Wong Kim Ark was born in the United States to Chinese immigrant parents. The government tried to deny his right to US citizenship.

Citizenship by birth on American soil was officially determined during the 1898 Supreme Court case *United States v. Wong Kim Ark*. Wong Kim Ark was born to Chinese parents in San Francisco, California. His parents were legal residents at the time, but they could not become US citizens. They later went back to China, leaving their son in the United States. As an adult, Wong traveled to China to visit his parents, but on returning to the United States, he was stopped and told he wasn't an American citizen. The government said that citizenship could not be extended to people of Chinese descent because of the Chinese Exclusion Act. Wong's case was brought before the Supreme Court, which reaffirmed the promise of the Fourteenth Amendment that all people born on American soil, regardless of race or ethnic background, are American citizens. Since he was born in the United States, Wong Kim Ark was therefore a citizen. The court also declared that "the Fourteenth Amendment to the Constitution is not confined to the protection of citizens" but rather applies to all people on US soil.[6]

How the Fourteenth Amendment Affects America Today

People still debate the Fourteenth Amendment today. Is it right to allow children born on American soil to automatically be citizens? How does it work?

A baby born on American soil is a citizen, regardless of the citizenship status of their parents. Some people think that if noncitizen parents have a baby in the United States—for example, while traveling on a tourist visa—the parents may then use the baby's citizenship to stay in America. These children are sometimes

The phrase "illegal immigrants" is used by some people to talk about undocumented immigrants, but many people believe it's offensive.

Women's Suffrage: The Fourteenth Amendment Declared that Women Are People

After the Civil War, the Fourteenth Amendment granted all people born on American soil citizenship, and therefore equal rights, such as voting. However, the second part of the amendment discussed voting as an exclusively male right. In fact, married women were considered property of their husbands and unable to make their own decisions. In 1875, in the case *Minor v. Happersett,* the Supreme Court found that women were American citizens under the amendment, but they were not allowed to vote. Women's rights advocates later cited this amendment in their fight to vote. They claimed that as citizens, they had the right to do so, and they were finally granted this right in 1920.[7]

known as "anchor babies," although many people consider this term to be offensive. However, having a child on US soil does not automatically allow noncitizen parents to stay in the country. While it's true that the child, as a US citizen, can ultimately serve as a sponsor if his or her parents apply for citizenship, the child cannot do this until reaching the age of twenty-one. In the meantime, the child's parents have no legal right to stay in the country by virtue of having a child who is a US citizen.[8]

Many recent cases regarding this issue have involved children born to undocumented immigrants. When they are born on US soil, the children are afforded citizenship rights under the Constitution, but their parents are not. If the parents are discovered, they can be deported, and the child may go into the foster care system or to any legal relatives who can take them. The child cannot sponsor the parents to come back into the country until he or she is twenty-one years old. It is a very difficult process because people who have been deported face penalties for being in the country illegally, such as a ten-year ban.[9] People today argue about whether children born to undocumented immigrants are truly citizens, but for now, the law remains in effect. Amendments are intentionally very difficult to change, and as such, it's unlikely that the law will change anytime soon.

A child who was born in a different country and brought over to America by his or her parents is not a citizen and can be deported. It is difficult for them to become citizens. Under a government program called Deferred Action for Childhood Arrivals (DACA), if children fit specific guidelines, they may apply for deferred action, meaning they won't be deported for two years and can apply for permission to work or study in the country. If they want to stay longer than two years, they can apply to extend their deferral.[10] Guidelines include being under the age of sixteen when they entered the country, being in school or having graduated already, and having no felonies. Some politicians are opposed to DACA, and battles have been fought in the courts over this program. The future of DACA remained uncertain as of summer 2019.

The Thirteenth Amendment prohibits slavery, and the Fourteenth Amendment says that all people born in the United States are citizens and are entitled to all rights given to citizens. Additionally, since the Fourteenth Amendment says that "people"—not "citizens"—are entitled to due process, it allows immigrants to be granted basic rights and trials, even if they are undocumented.

The Amendments and Immigration

In 2009, a woman named Christina Bebawy took part in a Bible lesson in Morocco. Police raided her apartment and she and the others in the lesson were thrown in jail and tortured. In Pakistan, a man named Zahid Ali was beaten for being a Zikri Muslim, a minority Muslim sect looked down upon by the majority. Joël Kangudi wrote a song criticizing the human rights violations of the government of the Democratic Republic of the Congo, and he was tortured when they found out.[1] What do these people have in common? All of them fled their countries and came to America, seeking the freedom to practice their own religion and speak their opinions freely.

Religious freedom and freedom of speech are only two of the many reasons why people come to the United States. Other reasons include escaping a tyrannical government, a country that forbids gay or transgender rights, a country where they can be arrested and held without due process, or domestic or gang violence. Most immigrants are simply seeking a safer life for their families. They want the freedoms that the Bill of Rights promises, especially those of the First, Fifth, and Sixth Amendments.

The First Amendment

The First Amendment says, "Congress shall make no law respecting an establishment of religion, or prohibiting the free exercise thereof; or abridging the freedom of speech, or of the press; or the right of the people peaceably to assemble, and to petition the government for a redress of grievances." This means that the amendment protects freedom of speech, freedom of religion, freedom of the press, and freedom to assemble.[2]

Freedom of speech means people may say anything they like—even openly criticize the government—without fear of punishment from the government. This freedom is denied in many countries, where people can be arrested, attacked, or executed for speaking their views. It includes the freedom to say things others may find rude or cruel but excludes threats of violence, and it only protects someone from being arrested; it doesn't protect them from retaliation from a private company. For example, someone can be fired from their job for saying things the company doesn't like.

In Pakistan in 2012, Malala Yousafzai was riding a bus home from school. She was twelve years old and already an activist for women's rights. She wrote a blog about her difficulty in getting an education as a girl in Pakistan. The Taliban, infuriated by her words, shot her in the head. She miraculously survived and left the country to continue her work.[3] Many people like her may seek life in a different country if they are punished for speaking against their government, and the First Amendment protects their right to criticize the American government.

Malala Yousafzai was shot by the Taliban after advocating for equal rights for girls and women in Pakistan.

Freedom of religion is the right to practice any religion a person chooses. It means that the government may not prevent anyone from or force anyone to practice a religion. The government may have prayer meetings if they choose, but it may not demand that anyone participate. The amendment appeals to immigrants who seek to practice their own religion or leave somewhere that forces them to follow a religion they don't believe in.

Freedom of the press means the right to circulate opinions in print without government censorship. People have the right to spread news and ideas in print, such as newspapers, magazines, and websites, without government interference. Some governments in the world limit or deny people access to news outside of government-run sources. People who wish to have the freedom to write their own opinions or seek a wider range of news value this freedom.

Freedom to assemble means that people may organize into groups and protest or march without government interference as long as they do not cause damage or commit acts of violence. Some restrictions apply to this right; for example, if the group wants to march in the street, they need a permit. However, many local governments have rules against denying someone a permit simply because they don't agree with their cause. No matter how others feel about the protest, as long as it does not cause damage, people may march for whatever cause they like.

The First Amendment makes the United States a particularly enticing country to immigrants, especially those from countries where the rights it grants are restricted.

The Fifth Amendment

In many countries, people can be arrested at the government's whim, and they may not be given a trial. Even if they are, many trials of this sort do not have a jury. In America, people

The Chinese Exclusion Act and the Immigration Act of 1924 severely limited the ability of Chinese and Japanese people to enter the United States.

are guaranteed a jury trial of impartial peers rather than being judged by the police or the government.

The Fifth Amendment says, "No person shall be held to answer for a capital, or otherwise infamous crime, unless on a presentment or indictment of a grand jury, except in cases arising in the land or naval forces, or in the militia, when in actual service in time of war or public danger; nor shall any person be subject for the same offense to be twice put in jeopardy of life or limb; nor shall be compelled in any criminal case to be a witness against himself, nor be deprived of life, liberty, or property, without due process of law; nor shall private property be taken for public use, without just compensation." This amendment means people don't have to speak about what they were accused of if they don't want to, and they cannot be forced to testify in their own trial. They also may not be tried twice for the same exact crime, using the exact same facts, after they've been found innocent.

People cannot be held indefinitely without a trial, and they cannot have their own property taken away.[4]

This amendment was key to immigrants who were fighting against the Chinese Exclusion Act in the 1800s.[5] People said they had been punished unfairly and their personal property was taken, even though they had not broken any laws. They said that despite being protected under the law, they were victims of cruel and unusual punishment. The amendment gives immigrants leverage to be allowed due process and to keep their property.

However, deportation is not considered a punishment. In the 1893 case of *Fong Yue Ting v. United States*, Fong Yue Ting and two others were detained under the 1892 Geary Act for not having the proper certificates. They were to be deported without a hearing. The Supreme Court ruled that while they had the right to a trial before being punished, deportation was a safety measure, not a punishment.[6]

Justice Horace Gray said that "every sovereign nation" has the power to deport noncitizens, and that was "as absolute and unqualified as the right to prohibit and prevent their entrance into the country."[7] That means that the government—often the executive branch or Congress—can deport people when they feel it's necessary, and they may change laws that apply to immigrants accordingly. While people are afforded rights under the Constitution, there is flexibility

In 2018, tensions at the US-Mexico border increased when asylum seekers clashed with those tasked with implementing new policies from the Trump administration.

The freedom of speech allows people to speak out against government policies they may disagree with, including immigration policies.

Asylum Seekers and Due Process

People from any country may seek asylum in the United States if they feel their lives are in danger in their home country. People seeking asylum must apply within a year of arriving, and they have the right to a trial. Individuals seeking asylum aren't citizens, but they are people and are therefore granted rights under the Constitution. Those who do not arrive at an authorized port of entry may be subject to expedited removal, but they still are allowed a trial. A backlog in the immigration court system has left many asylum seekers in limbo, however. In 2018, around 690,000 people were awaiting their hearings in immigration court.[8] By May 2019, pending cases had approached 1 million.[9]

in how the law is interpreted and what is considered a punishment.

The Sixth Amendment

Another amendment deals with the right to due process. The Sixth Amendment says, "In all criminal prosecutions, the accused shall enjoy the right to a speedy and public trial, by an impartial jury of the state and district wherein the crime shall have been committed, which district shall have been previously ascertained by law, and to be informed of the nature and cause of the accusation; to be confronted with the witnesses against him; to have compulsory process for obtaining witnesses in his favor, and to have the assistance of counsel for his defense." This amendment means that all people, citizens or not, have the right to an impartial jury trial held as quickly as possible after they're accused. They have the right to defend themselves and know who might testify against them. They also have the right to a lawyer and to know exactly what they're being accused of.[10]

Because they are people under the law, undocumented immigrants also have these rights. Immigrants who enter the United States illegally and are detained have the right to be properly processed by the police, not to testify if they so choose, and the right to an impartial trial. These rights are also granted to asylum seekers. However, just because something is a right doesn't always mean it's automatically granted; sometimes people have to ask for the things the Constitution grants them.

The rights outlined in this chapter are widely sought after. They make America an appealing place for people who are threatened by their government or their society in their home country. Anyone who enters the country is guaranteed these rights under the Constitution and Bill of Rights, though some of the interpretation of the laws may vary.

How Does Immigration Work?

People from all over the world wish to come to America to seek work, health care, and decent wages; to find a better life; or to gain freedom from government overreach. However, it's not as easy as simply crossing the border. So, how does immigration to America work?

The Immigration Process: Visas and Green Cards

Immigrants wishing to live in the United States and work or study require a visa. Visas can be obtained from US embassies in other countries. Many visas—such as travel, student, performer, and some work visas—are temporary. That means the person is a resident alien, and they may only stay as long as their visa lasts. In addition, the visa is limited. For example, a person who wishes to study at an American university requires a student visa. People on student visas may only study; they may not work or make any kind of income. Once they have completed their degree, they must leave immediately or apply for another type of visa. When a visa expires, the person is considered an undocumented immigrant and may be deported.

Immigration and citizenship in the United States are not always straightforward matters, especially given that policies can change when a new president is elected.

More permanent visas include those provided to spouses of American citizens, international children adopted by American parents, family members of citizens and residents, some translators, some employer-sponsored visas for long-term work, and diversity visas.[1] Diversity visas are a yearly pool of 50,000 visas for people from countries with few immigrants already in the United States. Recipients are picked randomly from a waiting list. The goal of these visas is to increase US diversity.

A green card is different from a visa because it allows the person to enter and stay for an unlimited amount of time.[2] A green card allows an immigrant to work, and it grants the holder many rights of citizenship, although not all. For example, a green card holder does not have the right to vote or be on a jury.

Citizenship

Immigrants who want to become American citizens must apply for citizenship. This process is called naturalization. People may apply for citizenship if they have been a resident alien for five years, or three years if they are married to a citizen. Members

Immigrants who want to become US citizens must apply. The process involves security screenings and a citizenship test.

Does Marriage to a US Citizen Give a Person Citizenship?

It's a common misconception that marrying an American citizen automatically makes someone a citizen. It does not. It does, however, make the immigrant more eligible for a green card. The person becomes "immediate family," which removes them from the waiting list of immigrants wanting green cards and speeds the process up. A resident alien needs to adjust their paperwork; a spouse overseas needs a special visa. If an undocumented immigrant marries a legal citizen, special government dispensation is required and is difficult to get. Once the immigrant has a legal green card, they may apply for citizenship after three years rather than five.[4]

of the military or children born abroad who have an American citizen as a parent may also be expedited.

It's a difficult process that involves a great deal of paperwork, interviews, security screenings, and a citizenship test. The test includes a written component on American history and civics, and a test of English-language reading, writing, and speaking skills. Applicants who make it through the process take the Oath of Citizenship, and from then on they are granted all the rights of a citizen.[3] Some countries, such as Sweden, allow people to remain citizens of both their home country and America. This is known as dual citizenship. Other countries, such as Japan, require people to renounce, or give up, their prior citizenship. This process can take as little as a year or as long as decades. An immigration lawyer can speed up the process, and certain people, such as the spouses of citizens or members of the military, are given priority.

Asylum Seekers

Asylum seekers are a special category of immigrant. These are people who come to the country seeking freedom from a tyrannical government or violence. They can apply for asylum if they fear living in their own country due to their religion, race, nationality, political alignment, or membership in a group that is being persecuted. Applying for asylum is free, but it must be done within one year after the person arrives in the United

In 2017, the Trump administration enacted new travel policies when many travelers were already en route to the United States.

States.[5] Spouses and unmarried children under twenty-one may also be included.

People waiting for asylum must get special permission to work. They may be granted a long-term visa, but they must go through a trial first. Entering the country undocumented isn't illegal if the person is seeking asylum and crosses at an official border checkpoint. If it is granted, they can apply for a green card and proceed toward citizenship if they wish. They are immediately eligible to work once they have asylum.

Legal versus Illegal Immigration

Visas, green cards, asylum, and naturalization are the legal paths to immigration. What happens if someone comes over the

border without the proper permits? Immigrants considered to be "illegal" are known as undocumented immigrants. It means that while they still have basic constitutional rights, they may be detained and are not legally allowed to work. If they are detained, they have the right to a trial to determine whether they should be deported, imprisoned, freed, or given a visa.

If they are detained, they are to be held for a "reasonable amount of time." In 2001, that amount of time was ninety days. At that time, a Supreme Court case presented an interesting problem. The case of *Zadvydas v. Davis* was heard in the Supreme Court.[6] The case involved a pair of immigrants, Kestutis Zadvydas and Kim Ho Ma, who both had committed

In Texas, temporary shelters house immigrants as they come across the US-Mexico border.

crimes. However, their countries of origin, Lithuania and Cambodia, would not take them back.

While the country tried to determine what to do with them, they were held past the ninety-day point. Zadvydas filed a writ of habeas corpus, or a complaint of unlawful detainment. His case reached the Supreme Court. The court ruled that the due process clause of the Fourteenth Amendment applies to all aliens in the United States, including those whose presence may be or is "unlawful, involuntary or transitory," reaffirming that undocumented immigrants are granted rights as people and are guaranteed a trial held as quickly as possible. The court acknowledged that the government could hold an alien longer than ninety days if deportation was possible in the future, but it ruled that "once removal is no longer reasonably foreseeable, continued detention is no longer authorized by statute," and the person must be released.[7] Part of the issue with this case was vague language. Under the Fifth Amendment, the law permits "reasonable detention," but the length isn't defined; in *Zadvydas*, the Supreme Court considered it to be about six months. The ruling released Zadvydas, as well as several thousand more detained immigrants. The decision is still contentious today as the country continues to debate how long people can be reasonably detained before it's considered a violation of their rights.

Studies say that about 44 percent of undocumented immigrants are visa overstays, which means people enter on a legal visa and don't leave when it expires. The Department of Homeland Security (DHS) estimated that there were about 12 million undocumented immigrants living in the United States as of 2015, or about 3.3 percent of the general population.[8] DHS also estimated that while the number of undocumented immigrants increased by 470,000 every year from 2000 to 2007, they increased by only 70,000 per year from 2010 to 2015. This shows that illegal immigration has decreased over time. Most undocumented immigrants are from Mexico.[9]

Unaccompanied minors—people under eighteen who do not come with family—also attempt to cross the border each year; in 2018, there were approximately 50,000 of them. Many are fleeing violence in Guatemala, Honduras, and El Salvador. The government is required to take custody and care for them under the William Wilberforce Trafficking Victims Protection Reauthorization Act of 2008. Those children are to be processed and then sent to foster care, allowed to live with an American relative if available, or deported back to their home country.[10]

Six states—California, Texas, Florida, New York, New Jersey, and Illinois—are home to 58 percent of undocumented immigrants.[11] Though they are not legally allowed to work, most find jobs in areas such as agriculture, construction, transportation, service industries, and manufacturing.[12] Twenty-six percent of them work in agriculture, such as picking crops. Companies hire undocumented immigrants for a variety of reasons. They're cheaper to hire, are less likely to argue or create trouble, cannot form a union or demand other rights, and tend to come with higher stakes: If they lose their jobs, they'll likely be deported. Many have debts that need to be paid or families to take care of. They are willing to work in conditions that legal workers are not, often for less money. Fear of being deported back to the circumstances they were trying to escape may motivate them as well.

People have a multitude of reasons for leaving their homes and immigrating to America. Documented and undocumented immigrants come for the same reasons: to flee violence, to look for freedom, to get better jobs or health care, or to further their education. All of them face a long road to residency or citizenship in the United States.

Immigration Today

America is still debating immigration. Much of the debate revolves around immigrants from Mexico, Central America, and the Middle East. Bans are currently in place and detention levels have risen. The DHS took over for the Bureau of Immigration in 2002, under the Homeland Security Act. Immigration and Customs Enforcement (ICE) is the largest department within DHS, and it handles things such as border control, immigration, customs, and trade.[1] It also handles deportation of immigrants.

Syrian Refugees

In March 2011, Syrian demonstrators criticizing human rights abuses began to protest against President Bashar al-Assad. The president's forces responded with violence, and demonstrations escalated. Violence rapidly intensified on both sides, creating

Many refugees from the Syrian civil war have found a temporary home in Turkey, but the ongoing war has influenced US policy when it comes to dealing with immigrants and refugees from Muslim-majority countries.

a civil war. Half a million people have died, with another 1.5 million permanently disabled.[2]

Displaced by this violence, 11 million people have fled Syria in search of safety. Of those, 93 percent are now in Turkey,

In 2017, President Trump increased the number of ICE officers at the US-Mexico border by 10,000, citing high numbers of immigrants. Shown here is a group of migrants waiting to enter the country to seek asylum.

Lebanon, and Jordan, and others are in Europe. Some sought asylum in America.

In 2017, President Trump was concerned that refugees from the Middle East would bring in crime and terrorism. This resulted in an executive order blocking people from seven primarily Muslim countries—Iran, Iraq, Syria, Yemen, Somalia, Sudan, and Libya—from entering the United States for ninety days. The order stopped all Syrian refugees from seeking asylum. This was the first version of the policy sometimes known as the "Muslim Ban." It was later amended, changing the list of affected countries to Iran, Libya, Syria, Somalia, Yemen, and North Korea. A limited number of people from Venezuela were included as well. Trump claimed these countries have a larger number of terrorist connections and are therefore dangerous. The revised policy was upheld by the Supreme Court and remains in effect as of 2019.[3]

Like the quota system of the past, the ban prevents any visas from being issued to those countries, with limited exceptions.

This greatly reduced the number of people who could seek safety in the United States. In 2017, America granted asylum to 3,024 Syrian refugees—about a fifth as many as had been admitted the previous year. In the first three months of 2018, only eleven Syrian refugees were let in.[4] Debate continues today about whether these refugees are dangerous and how many of them America should help as the Syrian war rages on.

The Border Crisis

Immigrants from Mexico and other parts of Central and South America continue to come to the southern US border. President Trump declared a national emergency in February 2019 for what he described as a "border crisis," which was the idea that masses of undocumented immigrants continue to cross the border illegally, increasing the drug trade and raising crime rates. Trump increased ICE by about 10,000 officers in 2017, in order to locate and deport undocumented immigrants.[5] Advocates for immigration say that a system called "metering"—which places a daily limit on the number of people who can apply for asylum at legal ports of entry—has caused many families to cross illegally, especially in Arizona and New Mexico.[6] Most of them are fleeing violence, and waiting in border towns in Mexico for their turn to make an asylum claim can increase their risk for violence, so they are more likely to cross illegally.

When they are discovered, because all people have the right to a trial whether they are citizens or not, they are placed in detention centers. Families are often separated from each other for months on end and live in very poor conditions.[7] As more immigrants come in and need to be held, the detention centers expand. The courts continue to be inundated with cases, and the backlog increases. Critics argue that this type of detention is cruel and unusual punishment and that it violates constitutional rights. The government argues that it has the

Immigrant Camps and Family Separation

Every immigrant who enters the United States is guaranteed due process. Because of this, immigrants need a place to wait. While some are placed with sponsor families, many are placed in camps. Children are often separated from their families, sometimes for months. Detainees report poor conditions such as too little food and overcrowded cells, and children often suffer from anxiety and depression.[8] While these camps have been in operation from many years under previous presidents, they were greatly expanded under the Trump administration. A greater number of people are seeking entry, and the system is backlogged by several hundred thousand cases.

right to detain an immigrant for as long as necessary under the 1996 Illegal Immigration Reform and Immigrant Responsibility Act. The Supreme Court ruled on this in 2018 in the case of *Jennings v. Rodriguez*, deciding that aliens are not guaranteed bond hearings nor is there a time limit on detention.[9]

The Border Wall

During President Trump's campaign, he promised to build a wall across the Mexican border that was about 2,000 miles (3,200 kilometers) long. Trump claimed that the United States needed this border wall to reduce the flow of undocumented immigrants, drugs, and crime that come into Texas, Arizona, and other nearby states, despite the fact that nearly half of all undocumented immigrants overstay their visas rather than cross the border.[10]

President Trump promised to build a new wall across the US-Mexico border and said that Mexico would pay for it. Mexico refused.

After failing to secure the $5.7 billion needed in funding from the Senate and House, President Trump shut the government down in December of 2018 and declared a state of emergency in 2019, which allowed him to go around Congress to access funds and move forward with building the wall. Since the definition of "emergency" in the law is not specific, he was able to move forward. The government is still in disagreement about whether the declaration will stand, how long it will take to build the wall, how it will be constructed, and how much it will ultimately cost to build and maintain.

Whether or not the wall will be effective is also still under debate. Trump argues that "only a Wall, or Steel Barrier, will keep our Country safe."[11] Supporters believe the wall will keep people from walking or riding over the border. They claim that it will reduce violence and the drug trade. Opponents of the wall say that the money could be better spent elsewhere, and they do not believe a wall will solve the immigration problem. A poll conducted in January 2019 by Quinnipiac University showed that while most Americans believed there was a border crisis, 59 percent believed that the wall would not solve the problem and would be a waste of money, though most approved of immigration security measures aside from the wall.[12] Of those polled, 88 percent of Republicans wished to build the wall, while 92 percent of Democrats and 59 percent of independents did not.[13]

As the debate about the success and cost of the wall continues, time will tell if the wall will be effective in solving immigration problems.

DACA

Enacted June 15, 2012, Deferred Action for Childhood Arrivals (DACA) is a program that allows undocumented people who were brought into the United States as children to remain in the country. In order to qualify, they must have entered the country when they were under sixteen years old and remained here, be in school or have graduated or be in the military, and not have been convicted of a felony.[14] While it's not a path to citizenship, it does allow them to stay in the country, and some may apply for residence. It allows them to get driver's licenses, enroll in school, get jobs, and serve in the military without fear of deportation. As of 2019, DACA protects about 700,000 immigrants.[15]

In September 2017, Trump said he would phase out DACA. Many lawsuits followed. On January 9, 2018, the US Appeals Court in California halted the termination of DACA. This required the DHS to take DACA renewal applications, meaning those who already had protection under DACA could apply to have it extended.[16] However, people who had never had DACA

In 2017, Trump decided to phase out the DACA program, which was created to protect people brought to the United States as children. This led to more protests and rallies, with much of the American public still supporting immigrants.

status could no longer apply for it. This process will remain until the lawsuits are settled, likely before the Supreme Court.

Supporters of DACA say that since the recipients were brought to the country by their parents instead of by their own choice, they should not be penalized for being undocumented.

They argue that DACA recipients have spent most of their lives in the United States, and they deserve to stay. Since they've been educated and gotten jobs in America, they have become part of the culture and contribute to it. In addition, they may not have a life to return to in their parents' country. Those who do not support DACA say that President Barack Obama overreached with his power in 2012 when he created the policy and that there should be a better way to deal with undocumented children. Many of them feel, however, that other immigration issues are more important and should be dealt with before DACA is discussed.[17]

Where Do We Go from Here?

Overall, Americans support immigration. In the Quinnipiac University survey, 73 percent of Americans said that immigration is good for the country's culture and economy. Immigration brings diversity and new resources to blend with America's. Think about the rich diversity of races, nationalities, cultural influences, and ideas that immigrants have brought to the United States over the centuries.

The fate of DACA, the wall, the asylum seekers, and undocumented immigrants remains in heated debate. Time will tell what happens to them and where the country goes from here.

1865 The Thirteenth Amendment is ratified, officially ending slavery.

1868 The Fourteenth Amendment gives citizenship to all people born on American soil and grants them equal rights under the Constitution.

1870 The Fifteenth Amendment grants all men the right to vote. The Naturalization Act of 1870 allows only European and African people to become citizens; Asian people are excluded.

1882 The Chinese Exclusion Act says no new Chinese immigrants can enter the country. It is repealed in 1943.

1885 The Alien Contract Labor Law prevents companies from bringing in immigrants by promising jobs.

1891 The Bureau of Immigration is created to decide how to deal with immigrants.

1892 The immigration station at Ellis Island opens. The Geary Act requires that Chinese people carry identification certificates or face deportation and extends the Chinese Exclusion Act.

1893 The Supreme Court case *Fong Yue Ting v. United States* determines that deportation is not a punishment but rather a safety measure.

1920 The Nineteenth Amendment grants women the right to vote and full citizenship rights.

1924 The Immigration Act of 1924, or the National Origins Quota System, allows a set number of visas per country.

1952 The Immigration and Nationality Act of 1952 keeps the quotas but ends Asian exclusion.

1965 The Immigration and Nationality Act of 1965 ends the quota system and prioritizes people with family in America or special skills.

1986 The Immigration Reform Act adds amnesty for undocumented immigrants and more paths to citizenship.

1990 The 1990 Immigration Act increases the overall number of immigrants and encourages immigration from underrepresented countries.

1996 The Illegal Immigration Reform and Immigrant Responsibility Act creates penalties for immigrants who are in the country without a visa or who have committed a crime.

2002 The Homeland Security Act creates the Department of Homeland Security, which replaces much of the Immigration Bureau.

2008 William Wilberforce Trafficking Victims Protection Reauthorization Act requires DHS to take custody of unaccompanied minors that cross the border.

2012 Deferred Action for Childhood Arrivals (DACA) allows undocumented people who were brought into the United States as children to remain in the country.

2018 President Trump stops visa applications from Iran, Libya, Syria, Somalia, Yemen, North Korea, and some from Venezuela. The Supreme Court rules in *Jennings v. Rodriguez* that aliens are not guaranteed bond hearings nor is there a time limit on detention.

2019 The House passes a new DREAM Act, creating a path toward permanent lawful status for undocumented immigrants who came to the country as children and meet certain requirements.

Introduction

1. D'Angelo Gore and Lori Robertson, "Trump's 'Travel Ban' Doesn't Affect All Muslims," Factcheck.org, June 29, 2018, www.fact check.org/2018/06/trumps-travel-ban-doesnt-affect-all-muslims.

CHAPTER 1: Who Are Immigrants?

1. "Is There a Difference Between a Visa and a Green Card," HG.org, 1996–2019, accessed on August 15, 2019, www.hg.org/legal-articles/is-there-a-difference-between-a-visa-and-a-green-card-28885.

2. "U.S. Immigration Before 1965," History.com, September 14, 2018, www.history.com/topics/immigration/u-s-immigration-before-1965.

3. Ed Crews, "Voting in Early America," Colonial Williamsburg Foundation, accessed on August 15, 2019, www.history.org/foundation/journal/spring07/elections.cfm.

4. "Yick Wo v. Hopkins," Legal Information Institute, May 10, 1886, www.law.cornell.edu/supremecourt/text/118/356?qt-_none_=0#qt-_none_.

5. "U.S. Immigration Before 1965," History.com.

6. "The Constitution of the United States," accessed on August 15, 2019, constitutionus.com.

7. "The Bill of Rights," The Bill of Rights Institute, accessed on August 15, 2019, billofrightsinstitute.org/founding-documents/bill-of-rights.

CHAPTER 2: Nationality and Immigration

1. Tom Deignan, "National Family History Month: Irish Famine Refugee's Story of Arrival in America," Irish Central, October 9, 2018, www.irishcentral.com/roots/genealogy/irish-immigrants-america-writings.

2. "Ellis Island History," The Statue of Liberty-Ellis Island Foundation Inc., accessed on August 15, 2019, www.libertyellisfoundation.org/ellis-island-history#Policy.

3. Lorraine Boissoneault, "How the 19th-Century Know Nothing Party Reshaped American Politics," *Smithsonian*, January 26, 2016, www.smithsonianmag.com/history/immigrants-conspiracies-and-secret-society-launched-american-nativism-180961915.

4. Keith J. Bell, "Alien Contract Labor Law of 1885," accessed on August 15, 2019, immigrationtounitedstates.org/333-alien-contract-labor-law-of-1885.html.

5. "Milestones in the History of U.S. Foreign Relations: Chinese Immigration and the Chinese Exclusion Acts," Office of the Historian, accessed on August 15, 2019, history.state.gov/milestones/1866-1898/chinese-immigration.

6. "Ellis Island History," The Statue of Liberty-Ellis Island Foundation Inc.

7. "The Immigration and Nationality Act of 1952 (The McCarran-Walter Act)," Office of the Historian, accessed on August 15, 2019, history.state.gov/milestones/1945-1952/immigration-act.

8. "US Immigration Since 1965," History.com, February 7, 2019, www.history.com/topics/immigration/us-immigration-since-1965.

9. "Immigration Reform and Control Act of 1986 (IRCA)," US Citizenship and Immigration Services, September 29, 2016, www.uscis.gov/tools/glossary/immigration-reform-and-control-act-1986-irca.

10. Yoram Hazony, "How Americans Lost Their National Identity," *Time*, October 23, 2018. time.com/5431089/trump-white-nationalism-bible.

11. "Illegal Immigration Reform and Immigration Responsibility Act," Cornell Law School, accessed on August 15, 2019, www.law.cornell.edu/wex/illegal_immigration_reform_and_immigration_responsibility_act.

12. "US Immigration Since 1965," History.com.

CHAPTER 3: The Thirteenth and Fourteenth Amendments

1. "13th Amendment," History.com, August 21, 2018, www.history.com/topics/black-history/thirteenth-amendment.

2. "Historical Highlights: the Civil Rights Act of 1866," History, Art and Archives: United States House of Representatives, accessed on August 15, 2019, history.house.gov/Historical-Highlights/1851-1900/The-Civil-Rights-Bill-of-1866/.

3. "14th Amendment," History.com, November 9, 2009, www.history.com/topics/black-history/fourteenth-amendment.

4. "Equal Protection," Cornell Law School, accessed on August 15, 2019, www.law.cornell.edu/wex/equal_protection.

5. Evansville Bar Association, "Law Day: The 14th Amendment," *Courier & Press*, April 29, 2017, www.courierpress.com/story/opinion/2017/04/29/law-day-14th-amendment-and-immigration/100814424/.

6. "United States v. Wong Kim Ark," Oyez, March 19, 2019, www.oyez.org/cases/1850-1900/169us649.

7. Jone Johnson Lewis, "Women's Rights and the Fourteenth Amendment," *ThoughtCo*, June 4, 2018, www.thoughtco.com/womens-rights-and-the-fourteenth-amendment-3529473.

8. Amanda Taub, "What Everyone Gets Wrong About 'Anchor Babies,'" *Vox*, August 26, 2015, www.vox.com/2015/8/26/9211277/anchor-babies-good.

9. Ilona Bray, "Can the Child of an Undocumented Immigrant Become a U.S. Citizen?" Alllaw.com, accessed on August 15, 2019, www.alllaw.com/articles/nolo/us-immigration/can-child-undocumented-immigrant-become-citizen.html.

10. "Frequently Asked Questions," US Citizenship and Immigration Services, March 8, 2018, www.uscis.gov/archive/frequently-asked-questions.

CHAPTER 4: The Amendments and Immigration

1. Miriam Jordan, "What It Takes to Get Asylum in the US," *New York Times*, May 2, 2018, www.nytimes.com/2018/05/02/us/what-it-takes-to-get-asylum-us.html.

2. Richard Wolf, "What the First Amendment Protects—and What It Doesn't," *USA Today*, April 6, 2018, www.usatoday.com/story/news/politics/2018/04/06/what-first-amendment-protects-and-what-doesnt/469920002.

3. "Malala Yousafzai Biography," Biography.com, March 29, 2018, www.biography.com/people/malala-yousafzai-21362253.

4. Tom Head, "The Fifth Amendment: Text, Origins and Meaning," *ThoughtCo*, January 26, 2018, www.thoughtco.com/the-fifth-amendment-721516.

5. Daniel Fisher, "Does the Constitution Protect Non-Citizens? Judges Say Yes," *Forbes*, January 30, 2017, www.forbes.com/sites/danielfisher/2017/01/30/does-the-constitution-protect-non-citizens-judges-say-yes/#43dad26e4f1d.

6. Evan Taparata, "While the Supreme Court Considers Deportation Policy, the Roots of Deportation Itself Come from a Much Earlier Case," Public Radio International, June 15, 2016, www.pri.org/stories/2016-06-15/while-supreme-court-considers-deportation-policy-deportation-policy-has-its-roots.

7. Thomas Tandy Lewis. "Fong Yue Ting v. The United States," Immigration to the United States, accessed on August 15, 2019, immigrationtounitedstates.org/503-fong-yue-ting-v-united-states.html.

8. "Asylum in the United States," American Immigration Council, May 14, 2018, www.americanimmigrationcouncil.org/research/asylum-united-states.

9. "Backlog of Pending Cases in Immigration Courts as of May 2019," TracImmigration, accessed on August 15, 2019, trac.syr.edu/phptools/immigration/court_backlog/apprep_backlog.php (accessed July 10, 2019).

10. "Sixth Amendment,"Cornell Law School, accessed on August 15, 2019, www.law.cornell.edu/constitution/sixth_amendment.

CHAPTER 5: How Does Immigration Work?

1. "Directory of Visa Categories," US Department of State—Bureau of Consular Affairs, accessed on August 15, 2019, travel.state.gov/content/travel/en/us-visas/visa-information-resources/all-visa-categories.html.

2. "Is There a Difference Between a Visa and a Green Card," HG.org, accessed on August 15, 2019, www.hg.org/legal-articles/is-there-a-difference-between-a-visa-and-a-green-card-28885.

3. "Citizenship Through Naturalization,"US Citizenship and Immigration Services, accessed on August 15, 2019, www.uscis.gov/us-citizenship/citizenship-through-naturalization.

4. "How to Get Citizenship After Marriage to an American Citizen," Alllaw.com, accessed on August 15, 2019, www.alllaw.com/articles/nolo/us-immigration/how-get-green-card-after-marriage-citizen.html.

5. "Asylum," US Citizenship and Immigration Services, accessed on August 15, 2019, www.uscis.gov/humanitarian/refugees-asylum/asylum.

6. "Zadvydas v. Davis," Oyez, March 20, 2019, www.oyez.org/cases/2000/99-7791.

7. "Zadvydas v. Davis (99-7791)," Cornell University Law School, accessed on August 15, 2019, www.law.cornell.edu/supct/html/99-7791.ZO.html.

8. "Population Estimates Illegal Alien Population Residing in the United States: January 2015," DHS Office of Immigration Statistics, December 2018, www.dhs.gov/sites/default/files/ublications/18_1214_PLCY_pops-est-report.pdf.

9. Lori Robertson, "Illegal Immigration Statistics," Factcheck.org, January 2019, www.factcheck.org/2018/06/illegal-immigration-statistics.

10. Lauren Shapiro, "Surge of 'Unaccompanied Children,'" Factcheck.org, July 18, 2014, www.factcheck.org/2014/07/surge-of-unaccompanied-children/.

11. Jens Manuel Krogstad, Jeffrey S. Passel, and D'Vera Cohn, "5 Facts About Illegal Immigration in the U.S," Pew Research Center, November 28, 2018, www.pewresearch.org/fact-tank/2018/11/28/5-facts-about-illegal-immigration-in-the-u-s.

12. Jeffrey S. Passel and D'Vera Cohn, "Occupations of Unauthorized Immigrant Workers," Pew Research Center Hispanic Trends, November 3, 2015, www.pewhispanic.org/2016/11/03/occupations-of-unauthorized-immigrant-workers.

CHAPTER 6: Immigration Today

1. "Fact Sheets: ICE," US Immigration and Customs Enforcement, January 3, 2018, www.ice.gov/factsheets.

2. "Why Is There a War in Syria?" BBC, February 25, 2019, www.bbc.com/news/world-middle-east-35806229.

3. "Trump Travel Ban: What Does This Ruling Mean?" BBC, June 26, 2018, www.bbc.com/news/world-us-canada-39044403.

4. "The U.S. Has Accepted Only 11 Syrian Refugees This Year," National Public Radio, April 12, 2018, www.npr.org/sections/parallels/2018/04/12/602022877/the-u-s-has-welcomed-only-11-syrian-refugees-this-year.

5. Miriam Valverde, "Trump Signs Executive Order to Increase ICE Deportation Officers," Politifact, January 16, 2017, www.politifact.com/truth-o-meter/promises/trumpometer/promise/1440/triple-ice-enforcement.

6. "Behind The Border 'Crisis': More Migrant Families Risk Dangerous Remote Crossings," National Public Radio, February 15, 2019, www.npr.org/2019/02/15/695135985/behind-the-border-crisis-more-migrant-families-risk-dangerous-remote-crossings.

7. Dagmar R. Myslinska, "Living Conditions in Immigration Detention Centers," NOLO, 2018, www.nolo.com/legal-encyclopedia/living-conditions-immigration-detention-centers.html.

8. Caitlin Dickerson, "Detention of Migrant Children Has Skyrocketed to Highest Levels Ever," *New York Times*, September 12, 2018, www.nytimes.com/2018/09/12/us/migrant-children-detention.html.

9. "Jennings v. Rodriguez, 583 U.S. ___ (2018)," Justia, accessed on August 15, 2019, supreme.justia.com/cases/federal/us/583/15-1204.

10. Lucy Rodgers and Dominic Bailey, "Trump Wall—All You Need to Know About US Border in Seven Charts," BBC, March 6, 2019, www.bbc.com/news/world-us-canada-46824649.

11. Donald Trump (@realdonaldtrump), "A big new Caravan is heading up to our Southern Border," Twitter, January 15, 2019, 5:37 a.m., twitter.com/realdonaldtrump/status/1085154110108848128.

12. "U.S. Voters Back Dem Plan to Reopen Government 2-1, Quinnipiac University National Poll Finds; More U.S. Voters Say Trump TV

Address Was Misleading," Quinnipiac University Poll, January 14, 2019, poll.qu.edu/national/release-detail?ReleaseID=2592.

13. Jacob Pramuk, "Most Voters Believe There's a Border Crisis—but They Don't Think Trump's Wall Will Solve It," CNBC, January 15, 2019, www.cnbc.com/2019/01/15/voters-doubt-trump-border-wall-will-solve-immigration-issues-poll-says.html.

14. "Consideration of Deferred Action for Childhood Arrivals (DACA)," US Citizenship and Immigration Services, accessed on August 15, 2019, www.uscis.gov/archive/consideration-deferred-action-childhood-arrivals-daca.

15. Reuters, "US Appeals Court Rules Against Trump on DACA Immigration Program," CNBC, November 8, 2018, www.cnbc.com/2018/11/08/us-appeals-court-rules-against-trump-on-daca-immigration-program.html.

16. Grace Donnelly, "Donald Trump, DACA and the Arguments Being Made For and Against Immigration Reform," *Fortune*, January 25, 2018, fortune.com/2018/01/25/trump-daca-citizenship.

17. Donnelly, "Donald Trump, DACA and the Arguments Being Made For and Against Immigration Reform."

GLOSSARY

act A statute or law made by a legislative body such as Congress. Acts can expire or be changed more easily than the Constitution.

alien A foreign person who is not a citizen; aliens can be legally or illegally living in the country.

amendment An article added to the Constitution which causes it to change.

amnesty Forgiveness for a crime. In the context of immigration, amnesty refers to a policy that allows undocumented immigrants to remain in the country legally.

asylum When a person flees from their home country to escape war, a disaster, a tyrannical government, or religious persecution.

citizen A native or naturalized person who has full protection of the laws of the country.

deportation Removing someone from the country.

detention When the government holds someone in custody, often to wait for a trial.

green card A permit that lets a person legally live and work permanently in the United States.

immigrant Any person who comes to live in a country permanently.

nationalism The idea of supporting one's country and culture over others.

nativism The idea that immigrants threaten the lifestyle, culture, or ideas of native-born people.

US Constitution The document for all legal authority in the United States, written in 1787.

visa A certificate or stamp in a person's passport that allows the person to legally stay in a country.

BOOKS

Barrett Osbourne, Linda. *This Land Is Our Land: A History of American Immigration.* New York, NY: Abrams Books for Young Readers, 2016.

Rozman Clark, Tea. *Green Card Youth Voices: Immigration Stories from a Fargo High School.* Minneapolis, MN: Green Card Voices, 2017.

Yousafzai, Malala. *We Are Displaced: My Journey and Stories from Refugee Girls Around the World.* New York, NY: Little, Brown and Company, 2019.

WEBSITES

Library of Congress: Immigration
www.loc.gov/teachers/classroommaterials/presentationsand activities/presentations/immigration/index.html
Explore immigration from countries all over the world!

Scholastic: Immigration: Stories of Yesterday and Today
teacher.scholastic.com/activities/immigration
Explore Ellis Island, hear immigrants' stories, and find helpful charts about immigration over time.

The Statue of Liberty-Ellis Island Foundation
www.libertyellisfoundation.org
Explore the history of Ellis Island, the Statue of Liberty, and the immigrants they've welcomed over the years.

INDEX